W9-BWF-386

DATE DUE

MATHWORKS!

Using Math to SURVIVE in the Wild

by Hilary Koll, Steve Mills, and Jonny Crockett

GARETH STEVENS
GS
PUBLISHING
A Member of the WRC Media Family of Companies

Math and Curriculum Consultant:
Debra Voege, Science and Math
Curriculum Resource Teacher

Please visit our web site at: **www.garethstevens.com**
**For a free color catalog describing Gareth Stevens Publishing's
list of high-quality books and multimedia programs, call
1-800-542-2595 (USA) or 1-800-387-3178 (Canada).
Gareth Stevens Publishing's fax: (414) 332-3567.**

Library of Congress Cataloging-in-Publication Data

Koll, Hilary.
    Using math to survive in the wild / Hilary Koll, Steve Mills,
and Jonny Crockett. — North American ed.
        p. cm. — (Mathworks!)
    ISBN-10: 0-8368-6767-X — ISBN-13: 978-0-8368-6767-1 (lib. bdg.)
    ISBN-10: 0-8368-6774-2 — ISBN-13: 978-0-8368-6774-9 (softcover)
    1. Mathematics—Problems, exercises, etc.—Juvenile literature.
    2. Survival skills—Juvenile literature. I. Mills, Steve, 1955-
II. Crockett, Jonny. III. Title. IV. Series.
    QA43.K626   2006
    510.76—dc22   2006040564

This North American edition first published in 2007 by
Gareth Stevens Publishing
A Member of the WRC Media Family of Companies
330 West Olive Street, Suite 100
Milwaukee, Wisconsin 53212 USA

Technical Consultant: Jonny Crockett
Jonny established the Survival School, in Exeter, England, in
1997 (www.survivalschool.co.uk), to share his knowledge of
survival skills and his enthusiasm for bushcraft. Today, he
conducts survival courses in locations ranging from the
Sahara Desert to the Borneo rain forest.

Gareth Stevens Editor: Dorothy L. Gibbs
Gareth Stevens Art Direction: Tammy West

Photo credits (t=top, b=bottom, c=center, l=left, r=right)
Dave Tyler: 1, 4-5, 6-7, 8-9, 14-15, 18-19; Jonny Crockett 6, 15b, 22-23;
Free Nature Pictures: 10-11; Mayang Murni Adnin: 20-21; Fotosearch:
24-25; Dynamic Graphics Group/IT Stock Free/Alamy: 26-27.

Every effort has been made to trace the copyright holders
for the photos used in this book. The publisher apologizes,
in advance, for any unintentional omissions and would be
pleased to insert the appropriate acknowledgements in
any subsequent edition of this publication.

Printed in the United States of America

1 2 3 4 5 6 7 8 9 10 09 08 07 06

CONTENTS

HAVE FUN WITH MATH

How to Use This Book

Math is important in the daily lives of people everywhere. We use math when we play games, ride bicycles, or go shopping, and everyone uses math at work. Imagine you are hiking through a forest. Suddenly, you discover that you are lost! You may not realize it, but a survival expert would use math to stay alive. In this book, you will be able to try lots of exciting math activities as you learn how to protect yourself in nature and "live off the land." If you can work with numbers, measurements, shapes, charts, and diagrams, then you could SURVIVE IN THE WILD.

How does it feel to be lost in a forest?

Grab your survival kit and learn how to find shelter, warmth, clean water, and food in the great outdoors.

Math Activities

The survival clipboards have math activities for you to try. Get your pencil, ruler, and notebook (for figuring out problems and listing answers).

NAVIGATE USING A COMPASS

You are hiking through the countryside with three friends. When you stop for lunch, you look around and realize that you are not sure where you are. You see a church in the distance and use your compass to figure out that the church is directly north of your location. Looking at your map, you see only one picnic site, and it has a church to the North. To make sure of your position, you look around for other landmarks. In one direction, you see an electricity pylon and a large hill. In another direction, you see a barn and a rocky outcrop with a flat top. Now that you know where you are, you need to decide where to go next.

Survival Work

The DATA BOX on page 9 shows a grid of the surrounding countryside. Find your position at the picnic site, then use the grid and the compass to answer these questions.

1) In which compass direction from where you are do you see
   a) a dead tree?
   b) Lone Farm?
   c) the electricity pylon?
   d) Black Hill?
   e) Flat Rock?

2) An angle is a measure of turn. A quarter turn forms a 90° angle, called a right angle. A 45° angle is half of a right angle. If you are facing the church, to what angle, moving clockwise, would you turn to face
   a) Lone Farm?
   b) the dead tree?
   c) Black Hill?
   d) Flat Rock?

8

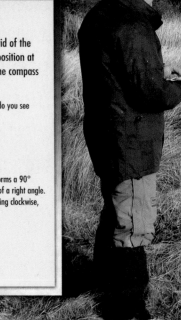

NEED HELP?

- If you are not sure how to do some of the math problems, turn to pages 28 and 29, where you will find lots of tips to help get you started.

- Turn to pages 30 and 31 to check your answers. (Try all the activities and challenges before you look at the answers.)

- Turn to page 32 for definitions of some words and terms used in this book.

Math Facts and Data

To complete some of the math activities, you will need information from a DATA BOX, which looks like this.

DATA BOX Grid of the Countryside

church

electricity pylon   Flat Rock

Black Hill   picnic site   Lone Farm

YOU ARE HERE   dead tree

NW N NE
W   E
SW S SE

Math Challenge

Green boxes, like this one, have extra math questions to challenge you. Give them a try!

Compass Facts

- A compass needle always points to magnetic north, but from place to place and year to year, magnetic north is in a slightly different direction.
- The difference between magnetic north and geographic north, which is north on a map, is called magnetic variation.

A map and a compass will keep you going in the right direction.

Math Challenge

1) Face Black Hill and turn 90° clockwise. What do you turn to face?

2) Face Flat Rock and turn 90° counter-clockwise. What do you turn to face?

3) Face Lone Farm and turn 45° counter-clockwise. What do you turn to face?

You will find lots of amazing details about survival skills and equipment in FACT boxes that look like this.

9

SURVIVAL KIT

Survival means "staying alive." That might sound easy to do, but, each day, people all over the world find themselves in situations where survival is not easy. What if you found yourself lost in a forest? How would you survive? Human beings need four main things to survive: shelter and warmth, to protect us from rain and cold weather, and clean water and food, to keep our bodies working properly. What would you do for shelter in a forest? How would you keep dry and warm? Where would you find clean water? What would you eat? What basic things could help keep you alive?

Survival Work

The DATA BOX on page 7 shows ten important items to include in a survival kit. Each item has a point value. The higher the point value, the more useful the item is in saving your life.

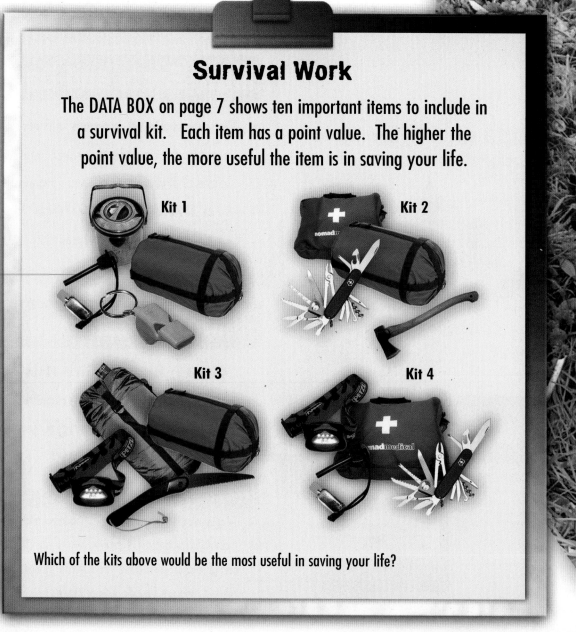

Kit 1

Kit 2

Kit 3

Kit 4

Which of the kits above would be the most useful in saving your life?

Items That Could Save Your Life

knife		17 points
saw		14 points
fire starter		13 points
cooking pot		11 points
axe		9 points
tent		8 points
sleeping bag		7 points
first aid kit		5 points
whistle		3 points
flashlight		1 point

Math Challenge

Use the DATA BOX above to find how many points you would have if you decided to take all of the items.

Equipment Facts

- A fire starter is sometimes called a "sparker" because it creates white-hot sparks that can light a fire. This tool produces sparks of about 5,500 °F.
- Some survival experts use tree branches to make shelters. Others use poles and a plastic sheet, but many just use regular tents.

Equipment Facts

- When you do not have a saw or an ax, even a sharp knife can help you build a shelter.
- To attract attention, blowing a whistle is better than shouting. When you shout, your voice carries only a few hundred yards, but a whistle can be heard more than half a mile away.

A survival kit must be light enough to carry easily.

NAVIGATE USING A COMPASS

You are hiking through the countryside with three friends. When you stop for lunch, you look around and realize that you are not sure where you are. You see a church in the distance and use your compass to figure out that the church is directly north of your location. Looking at your map, you see only one picnic site, and it has a church to the North. To make sure of your position, you look around for other landmarks. In one direction, you see an electricity pylon and a large hill. In another direction, you see a barn and a rocky outcrop with a flat top. Now that you know where you are, you need to decide where to go next.

Survival Work

The DATA BOX on page 9 shows a grid of the surrounding countryside. Find your position at the picnic site, then use the grid and the compass to answer these questions.

1) In which compass direction from where you are do you see
   a) a dead tree?
   b) Lone Farm?
   c) the electricity pylon?
   d) Black Hill?
   e) Flat Rock?

2) An angle is a measure of turn. A quarter turn forms a 90° angle, called a right angle. A 45° angle is half of a right angle. If you are facing the church, to what angle, moving clockwise, would you turn to face
   a) Lone Farm?
   b) the dead tree?
   c) Black Hill?
   d) Flat Rock?

Grid of the Countryside

church

electricity pylon

Flat Rock

Black Hill

picnic site

Lone Farm

YOU ARE HERE

dead tree

N
NW   NE
W   E
SW   SE
S

Math Challenge

1) Face Black Hill and turn 90° clockwise. What do you turn to face?

2) Face Flat Rock and turn 90° counter-clockwise. What do you turn to face?

3) Face Lone Farm and turn 45° counter-clockwise. What do you turn to face?

Compass Facts

• A compass needle always points to magnetic north, but from place to place and year to year, magnetic north is in a slightly different direction.

• The difference between magnetic north and geographic north, which is north on a map, is called magnetic variation.

A map and a compass will keep you going in the right direction.

NAVIGATE USING THE SUN

Your group sets off in a southeast direction. After walking a couple of miles, you find yourselves in a densely wooded area. There are trees all around so you need a compass to show you which way to go. You look for the compass, but you cannot find it! Someone must have dropped it back at the picnic site. Do you go all the way back to look for it, or do you know another way to keep you headed in the right direction? It is a sunny day — so you can use the Sun! In Earth's Northern Hemisphere, the Sun is in the South at midday. In the Southern Hemisphere, the Sun is in the North at midday.

Survival Work

You used the Sun and your watch to find which way is north. Now you and your friends are ready to move on. The coordinate grid in the DATA BOX on page 11 will help you. You are at coordinates (0, 3). Use the grid to answer these questions.

1) What are the coordinates of each of these locations
   a) Wooden Bridge?
   b) Canal Rocks?
   c) Ling Marsh?

2) What is at each of these coordinates?
   a) (4, 1)
   b) (5, 0)
   c) (5, 5)

Math Challenge

Look at the DATA BOX on page 11. You and your friends are at coordinates (0, 3) on the grid.

From your location, which place will you reach first if you travel
a) E?
b) SE?
c) NE?

How to Use a Watch to Find North

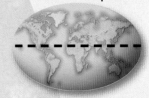

Northern Hemisphere

Southern Hemisphere

IF YOU ARE IN THE NORTHERN HEMISPHERE . . .
1) Point the hour hand of your watch toward the Sun.
2) Imagine a line halfway between the hour hand and the 12 on the watch.
   This line is the north/south line.
3) Remember that the Sun is in the east before midday and in the west after midday.
   Use this information to help you figure out which way is North.

IF YOU ARE IN THE SOUTHERN HEMISPHERE . . .
1) Point the 12 on your watch toward the Sun.
2) Imagine a line halfway between the 12 and the hour hand to give you
   the north/south line.
3) Remember that the Sun is in the east before midday and in the west after midday.
   Use this information to help you figure out which way is North.

DATA BOX Location Coordinates

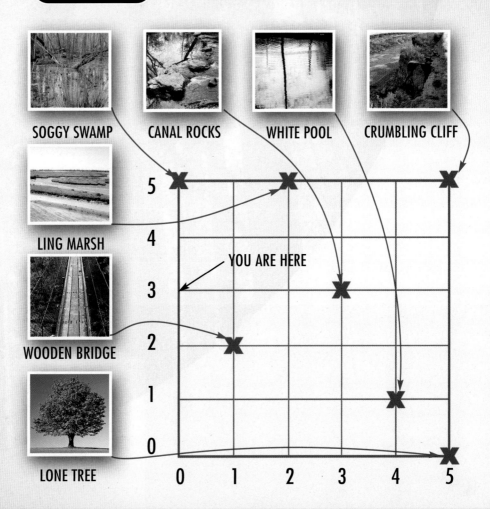

SOGGY SWAMP   CANAL ROCKS   WHITE POOL   CRUMBLING CLIFF

LING MARSH

YOU ARE HERE

WOODEN BRIDGE

LONE TREE

LOST IN THE FOREST

You and your friends decide to head for Wooden Bridge, but, now, it is late, and it is getting dark. You are lost in the forest! You all agree that it will be best to stay where you are overnight. In the few remaining hours of daylight, you need to plan how to survive the night. There are many things you could do. You could build a shelter or light a fire, but maybe you should look for water, hunt for food, or gather leaves to keep you warm. Because you want to stay together in one group, you will not have time to do everything. Which tasks should you pick? The light is fading fast, you must decide quickly.

Survival Work

The DATA BOX on page 13 has a table showing how long the various tasks might take and how useful each task is for helping you stay alive. Use this information to answer these questions.

1) Which jobs could you do in the four hours you have left before complete darkness? (Make sure that the jobs do not take more than four hours altogether.)

2) Exactly how long will it take to do the jobs you decide on? (Give your answer in hours and minutes.)

3) After you finish the chosen tasks, how much of the 4 hours will you have to spare?

SURVIVAL FACT

If you survive a plane crash or a car accident in the wilderness, stay with the wreckage. The wreckage is easier to find than a person wandering alone.

SURVIVAL FACT

When you are in a survival situation, you need to think about shelter, fire, water, and food. You have to decide which are most important for the environment you are in.

SURVIVAL FACT

To stay alive in the wild, you need to be fit and have the right equipment, knowledge, and skills to survive, but, most important, you need to have a positive mental attitude.

DATA BOX Survival Tasks

This table shows estimates of how much time the jobs listed might take to complete. The jobs are also graded from 1 to 10 on how useful they are, with 10 being very useful and 0 being useless.

Job		Time to Complete	Usefulness
hunt for food		210 minutes	6
build shelter		150 minutes	8
light a fire		45 minutes	9
look for water		105 minutes	7
gather leaves to to keep warm		150 minutes	5

Math Challenge

Use the time estimates in the DATA BOX above to answer these questions.

1) How much time would it take to do all of the jobs
   a) in minutes?
   b) in hours?

2) Doing two of the jobs takes 4¼ hours. Which jobs are they?

13

BUILDING A SHELTER

To find shelter for the night, you should look both for suitable places and for building materials. You might find a cave or a hollow tree that could provide shelter, but you also might have to build your own shelter. Look around to see what materials are available. If you are in a forest, you can use sturdy tree branches to form the basic shape of the shelter, but you will need to tie them together. What if you do not have any rope or string in your survival kit? What would you use instead? How will you make your shelter waterproof? Look at the box on page 15 to find out.

Survival Work

You have collected some branches for your shelter. You need many branches of several different lengths. You measure the branches in inches, but your friend measures them in feet.

Match pieces of wood that are the same length. Example: 84 inches = 7 feet

Your branches (in inches)				Your friend's branches (in feet)			
84	90	192	198	9	18	5.5	8
72	66	96	60	16.5	7.5	7	16
216	120	78	108	6.5	10	5	6

Math Challenge

Using your answers from the Survival Work, list the lengths of the branches in order of size, starting with the shortest.

SHELTER FACTS

Where you build a shelter is very important and will depend on where you are.
- In the jungle, you need to build a shelter off the ground to avoid snakes and other creepy crawlies.
- In the Arctic, you need to build a shelter below the surface to protect yourself from the wind.
- In the desert, you need to build a shelter to keep you out of the baking Sun.

How to Make a Shelter

1) Check the site you have chosen to make sure it is away from dangers such as falling branches or flooding. Also avoid areas that have lots of animal tracks.

2) Clear the area and plan your shelter carefully. For example, the wind should not blow straight into the shelter's opening.

3) Find a thick branch that is long enough to go between two trees. Tie it to the trees using rope, string, or roots.

4) Place thinner branches against the long branch to act as rafters. These branches should be long enough to form a shelter you can lie in comfortably.

5) Weave even thinner branches or long twigs in and out of the rafters to make the framework rigid.

6) Now cover the shelter. Use ferns, leaves, and pine branches. The covering should be several feet thick. You should also block the ends of the shelter to keep the wind out.

7) Lay some logs on the ground inside the shelter for a bed. You can cover them with the same materials you used to cover the shelter.

8) Light a fire next to the shelter to keep you warm.

This man is making the frame of a shelter.

LIGHTING A FIRE

One of the most important survival skills is knowing how to light a fire. Fire provides warmth, as well as light in the darkness. Most wild animals are afraid of fire so lighting a campfire will make your shelter safer. You can use fire to boil water, which is often necessary for making sure that water you find in the wild is safe to drink. You can use fire to cook food, too, so it will be warm and safe to eat. Lighting a fire can give a cold, tired group a morale boost, and smoke from a fire may attract rescuers. Fire is one of the most useful survival tools, so be sure to carry matches or a fire starter in your survival kit.

Survival Work

Each of these four different campfires has a circle of rocks around it.
Each rock measures 5 inches from end to end at its widest point.

⬭ = 5 inches

A

B

C

D

What is the approximate perimeter of each fire?

SURVIVAL FACTS

• The outer bark of a birch tree makes good kindling.
It peels off the tree easily, and it will light from a spark.
• A fire burns hotter when it is built in the shape of a pyramid.
The pyramid shape is good for getting a young fire going,
but when you want to cook, you need to make
the fire flatter to provide heat more evenly.

HOW TO BUILD AND LIGHT A FIRE

1) Collect tiny twigs, leaves, and bark for kindling. (Birch bark is very good.) If the kindling is damp, put it in your pocket to dry out.

2) Break off very thin, dead twigs from trees and bushes and put them in a pile. Then make a pile of bigger twigs that are about the size of pencils.

3) Make two more piles, one of large sticks and one of logs.

4) Decide where to build the fire. Make sure it is not too close to any low-hanging branches.

5) Dig a hole about 6 inches deep and about 12 inches in diameter.

6) Place green sticks in the bottom of the hole. They will keep the kindling off the damp ground and help the fire burn.

7) Add the kindling and set fire to it, using matches or a fire starter.

8) When the burning kindling has a strong flame, place the thinnest twigs on the fire. After these twigs start burning, place the bigger twigs, then the large sticks, and, finally, the logs on the fire, forming a pyramid shape.

9) Place smooth, round rocks, each about the size of a grapefruit, around the fire. The rocks will stop the fire from spreading.

Math Challenge

Sitting around the campfire, you and your friends carve small pieces of wood into these shapes. This kind of carving is called whittling.

1) Name each of the shapes.

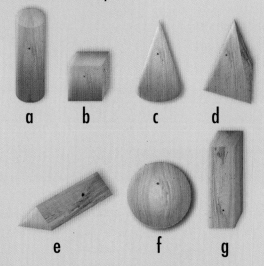

a b c d

e f g

2) How many faces and edges does shape b have?

3) What is the volume of a rectangular prism that is 6 inches long, 2 inches wide, and 3 inches high?

FINDING WATER

After you have shelter and a fire, your next priority is finding water. Without water or some other kind of liquid to drink, humans can normally survive for only about three days. Finding water in the wild is not always easy. Your group is lucky. You found a fast-flowing stream nearby, and you are boiling the water to make it safe to drink. Waiting for the water to boil, your group talks about other ways to collect water. Because some methods can be used only in sunny weather, and others need rain or boggy ground, you all agree that it is best to take enough water with you in the first place!

Survival Work

The DATA BOX on page 19 contains information about different ways to collect water in the wild. Use the information to answer these questions.

1) Using all four methods, how much water would collect?

2) Is this more or less than one quart?

3) Most health organizations say that an adult should drink between 1½ and 2½ quarts of water every day. Have you collected at least the minimum daily amount needed for one adult?

4) If you drank 1½ quarts of water every day, how many quarts would you drink in one week?

Math Challenge

You have two containers. One holds 3 quarts of water. The other holds 5 quarts of water.

How would you measure exactly 1 quart of water using both containers? (You are not allowed to half-fill the containers.)

DATA BOX

Collecting Water

You and your friends discuss four different ways to collect water in the wild.

METHOD 1

Tie pieces of cloth around your ankles and walk through a dew-covered field. The cloths will absorb the watery dew. Then squeeze the water out of the cloths.

Water collected: 4 ounces

METHOD 2

Dig into marshy or boggy ground to create a puddle of water. Use leaves and bark to scoop water out of the puddle. **Water collected: 3 ounces**

METHOD 3

On a hot, sunny day, tie clear plastic bags around leafy green twigs. Water will collect in the bottoms of the bags.

Water collected: 9 ounces

METHOD 4

Collect rainwater by tilting your shelter downward and letting the water run into a cooking pot.

Water collected: 32 ounces

When you are looking for a stream, remember that water travels downhill.

COLLECTING FOOD

People can live up to sixty days without food, so finding food usually is not one of the most important survival tasks. One of your friends, however, is feeling ill, and you think he might feel better if he eats something. You spot some mushrooms nearby, but because you cannot identify them, you leave them alone. You know you should not eat anything unless you are sure it is harmless. Some mushrooms are poisonous enough to kill people. As you look around for safe foods to eat, you see berries. Then you begin to notice lots of other foods. They are not the kinds of foods you eat at home, but they will keep you alive!

Survival Work

In the DATA BOX on page 21, you will see a pictograph that shows how many edible berries, roots, nuts, leaves, bugs, and flowers you collected. Use the pictograph to help you answer these questions.

1) Which kind of food did you collect the most of?

2) Which kind of food did you collect the least of?

3) How many flowers did you collect?

4) How many roots did you collect?

5) How many more leaves than berries did you collect?

6) How many more bugs than nuts did you collect?

FOOD FACTS

Do not be afraid to eat unusual items because of how you think they might taste. You might be surprised to know that
- Earthworms taste like bacon rind.
- Fish eyes contain fresh water and taste like fried egg yolks.
- Ant larvae taste like shrimp.

Math Challenge
How many edible food items did you collect all together?

Foods Found in the Wild

This pictograph shows the different kinds of edible foods you found in the wild and how much of each food item you collected.

berries

roots

nuts

leaves

bugs

flowers

PICTOGRAPH KEY

= 12 items

= 12 items

= 12 items

= 12 items

= 12 items

= 12 items

CROSSING A RIVER

You and your friends survive the night in the forest, successfully building a shelter, lighting a fire, collecting drinking water, and finding safe foods to eat. As dawn breaks, you continue on to Wooden Bridge. Unfortunately, after you reach the bridge, you see that it has completely collapsed and fallen into the river. All that remains on your side of the riverbank are a few pieces of wood. You still have to get across the river, but one of your friends cannot swim. How will you all get to the other side without being swept away by the current — or drowning? You cleverly decide to use the remaining pieces of the bridge to make a raft.

Survival Work

You successfully build a raft but then discover that only two people can travel on it at the same time.

One person must always be on the raft or it will float away down the river. What is the fewest number of times the raft will need to cross the river to get four people to the other side?

RAFT FACTS

- When you have to cross a river, a raft will keep you dry. If you swim, you will get cold and wet. It may be difficult for you to warm up again, which could be dangerous.
- Rafts are best for traveling down a river rather than just crossing it.
- When you cross a river, keep glancing upstream to make sure you are not hit by anything being washed downstream.

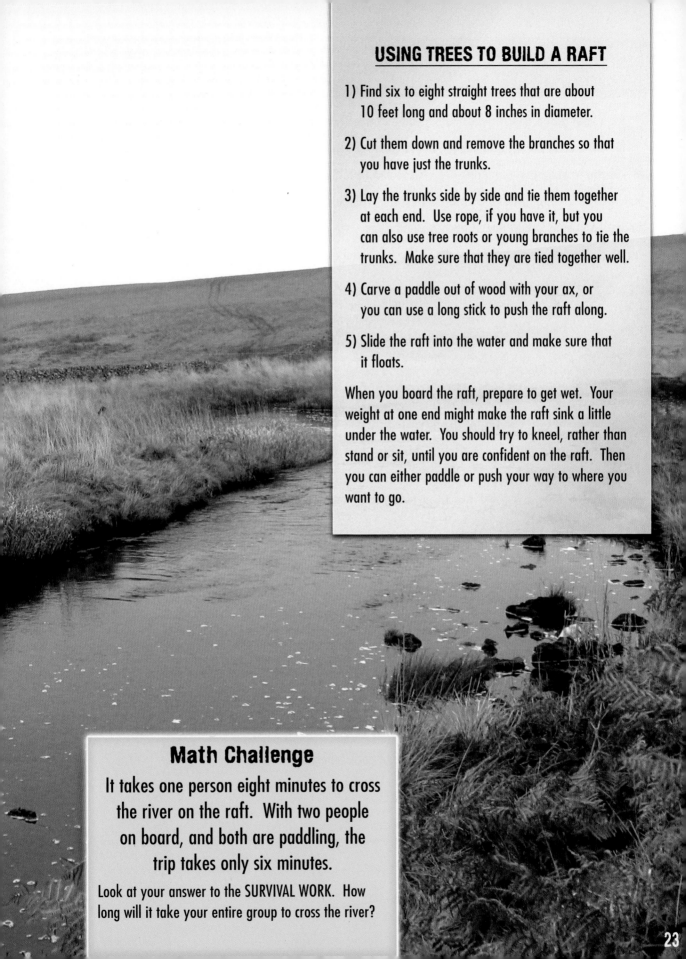

USING TREES TO BUILD A RAFT

1) Find six to eight straight trees that are about 10 feet long and about 8 inches in diameter.

2) Cut them down and remove the branches so that you have just the trunks.

3) Lay the trunks side by side and tie them together at each end. Use rope, if you have it, but you can also use tree roots or young branches to tie the trunks. Make sure that they are tied together well.

4) Carve a paddle out of wood with your ax, or you can use a long stick to push the raft along.

5) Slide the raft into the water and make sure that it floats.

When you board the raft, prepare to get wet. Your weight at one end might make the raft sink a little under the water. You should try to kneel, rather than stand or sit, until you are confident on the raft. Then you can either paddle or push your way to where you want to go.

Math Challenge

It takes one person eight minutes to cross the river on the raft. With two people on board, and both are paddling, the trip takes only six minutes.

Look at your answer to the SURVIVAL WORK. How long will it take your entire group to cross the river?

AVOIDING DANGER

As your group finally heads home, you talk about the difficulties and dangers you have faced. You were cold, thirsty, and hungry, but you solved all of these problems. You built a shelter and lit a fire to keep you warm and dry. You found water, and you gathered safe things to eat. You even managed to build a raft and cross a river safely. Your success was due in part to your awareness of the dangers and your knowledge of how to avoid them. Now you wonder what other dangers you might face during the rest of your trip. You and your friends come up with a list.

Survival Work

As your group discusses the list of dangers you might encounter, you decide that some of the dangers are more likely to occur than others. To best prepare for further dangers, you and your friends add to the list the likelihood of each danger happening.

a) quicksand	unlikely
b) hypothermia	very likely
c) hit by lightning	very unlikely
d) bridge collapse	even chance
e) tiger attack	impossible
f) snakebite	unlikely
g) fall from a cliff	even chance
h) cut with a knife	likely

Probabilities can be shown on a probability scale. Make a probability scale like the one below and mark the probability of each danger listed above on the scale.

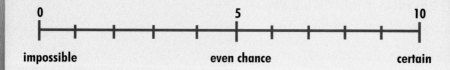

```
0                    5                   10
|--|--|--|--|--|--|--|--|--|--|
impossible        even chance        certain
```

More Survival Advice

- Use all your senses. Danger comes in many forms.
- Keep an eye out for the tracks of dangerous animals.
- Look for areas where leaves have been disturbed. The leaves might be covering a trap.
- When you cross over logs, always walk on the logs instead of stepping over them. There may be snakes on the other side.
- If you step into quicksand, stay calm. Take off your backpack, then lie on your back and, very slowly, try to swim with a backstroke to the side.
- If you go away from your camp for any reason, leave a note or signs that will let others know where you have gone.
- If you are lost, walk downhill. Water travels downhill so you should come to a stream. Follow the stream until you get to a river. Follow the river until you find a town, a farm, or houses.
- Look for tracks with the shapes of human feet, shoes, or boots. They can lead you back to civilization.
- When you get into a survival situation, make a plan and stick to it.

Math Challenge

Use the words "certain," "very likely," "likely," "even chance," "unlikely," "very unlikely," "impossible" to describe the probability of each of these events happening.

a) It will rain this week.
b) The sun will rise tomorrow.
c) A person in your family will be eaten by a wolf today.
d) The day after Monday will be Friday.
e) A newborn baby will be a boy.

SIGNALING

T he town you started from is almost in sight. Unfortunately, as you cross some rough ground, one of your friends falls and twists her ankle. She is not hurt too badly, but she cannot walk any further. She needs medical attention. The batteries on your cell phone have lost power, so how will you get help? Your group decides to split up. Two members of the group start walking the rest of the way to the town to get help, while you will wait with your friend. As you sit with her, you talk about what you would do if it was just the two of you. You would probably have to signal for help. Do you know the Morse code for SOS?

Survival Work

The DATA BOX on page 27 shows the signals for Morse code. Use the code to answer these questions.

1) If you used a whistle to send the message "SOS,"
   a) how many times would you blow the whistle?
   b) how many short blows?
   c) how many long blows?

2) How many times would you blow the whistle for
   a) come quickly? b) injured child? c) broken leg?
   How many short blows for each? How many long blows?

Small planes flying over remote areas carry smoke flares for signaling in an emergency.

Math Challenge

The International signal for distress is six long blows on a whistle every minute or six long flashes with a light every minute.

If you signaled with a whistle for one hour, how many times would you blow the whistle?

DISTRESS SIGNALS

If you do not have a whistle or a light, such as a flashlight, you will have to use other methods to attract attention or send a distress signal.

1) If you have a fire, you can use smoke to get attention. Smoke can be different colors. Black smoke comes from burning rubber. White smoke comes from burning leaves or green branches. It is important to think about which color smoke will show up the best in a given location. If you are in the desert, use black smoke. If you are in a forest, white smoke will show up better against the dark trees.

2) Use brightly colored clothing to signal with. Wave a jacket or, to signal a plane, spread the jacket out on the ground. Try to get up as high as possible to be seen more easily.

3) Use a mirror to reflect sunlight. Moving the mirror will make the light flash.

DATA BOX International Morse Code

Morse code is a way of sending messages using short and long sounds or flashes of light to represent letters and numbers.
A dot indicates a short sound. A dash indicates a long sound.

KEY TO INTERNATIONAL MORSE CODE

A •—	J •———	S •••	0 —————
B —•••	K —•—	T —	1 •————
C —•—•	L •—••	U ••—	2 ••———
D —••	M ——	V •••—	3 •••——
E •	N —•	W •——	4 ••••—
F ••—•	O ———	X —••—	5 •••••
G ——•	P •——•	Y —•——	6 —••••
H ••••	Q ——•—	Z ——••	7 ——•••
I ••	R •—•		8 ———••
			9 ————•

MATH TIPS

PAGES 6–7

TOP TIP: You can add small numbers in any order. Look for pairs of numbers that add to make 10.

Examples:
1 + 9 = 10   4 + 6 = 10
2 + 8 = 10   5 + 5 = 10
3 + 7 = 10

PAGES 8–9

Survival Work

An angle is a measure of turn. Angles are measured in degrees. The symbol for degrees is °. One whole turn, or complete revolution, is 360°. A quarter turn is 90°, or one right angle. One whole turn has four right angles. Half of a right angle is 45°.

one whole turn (one complete revolution) 360°

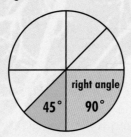

right angle
45°   90°

PAGES 10–11

Survival Work

To use coordinates to find a point on a grid, read, first, along the bottom of the grid, then up the side.

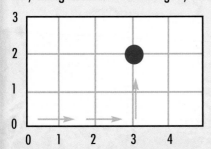

Example: For grid coordinates (3, 2), move 3 squares along the bottom, then 2 squares up to find the exact point.

PAGES 12–13

Survival Work

TOP TIP: One hour is 60 minutes so 4 hours is 4 x 60 (240 minutes). Multiply by 60 to change hours to minutes. Divide by 60 to change minutes to hours.

PAGES 14–15

Survival Work

To match lengths in inches with lengths in feet, you need to remember that 12 inches = 1 foot. To change inches to feet or feet to inches, you should know the 12 times table.

1 x 12 = 12   2 x 12 = 24
3 x 12 = 36   4 x 12 = 48
5 x 12 = 60   6 x 12 = 72
7 x 12 = 84   8 x 12 = 96
9 x 12 = 108   10 x 12 = 120

TOP TIP: To multiply larger numbers by twelve, add the answers to two smaller problems.

Example: To multiply 18 x 12, add the answers to 18 x 10 and 18 x 2.

```
   18        18        180
 x 10       x 2       + 36
  180        36        216
```

PAGES 16–17

Math Challenge

A **face** is a flat surface on a solid shape.

An **edge** is a line segment where two of the faces on a solid shape meet.

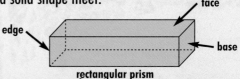

edge   face
                              base
rectangular prism

volume = length x width x height

The volume of a solid is labeled as cubic units, such as cubic inches or cubic feet.

28

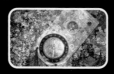
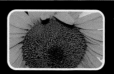

PAGES 18–19

Survival Work

TOP TIP: 1 quart = 32 ounces

Math Challenge

Think about filling the 3-quart container twice and the 5-quart container once.

PAGES 20–21

Survival Work

A pictograph should always have a key to tell you what each picture stands for. Each circle in this pictograph represents 12 of the items pictured. Half of a circle stands for 6 items.

Math Challenge

Review the 12 times table in the tips for pages 14–15.

PAGES 22–23

Survival Work

You might find it useful to draw the crossings.

(● = 1 person)

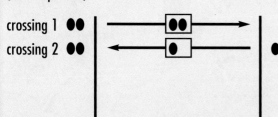

Remember that one person must always bring the raft back across the river to pick up another person.

PAGES 24–25

Survival Work

To show a certain probability, you can mark a cross on the scale (line). The cross on this scale shows a probability that is "likely" to happen.

impossible   even chance   certain

PAGES 26–27

Math Challenge

Remember that there are 60 minutes in 1 hour.

ANSWERS

PAGES 6–7

Survival Work

Kit 2 is the best. It is worth 38 points.
Kit 1 = 34 points. Kit 3 = 30 points.
Kit 4 = 36 points.

Math Challenge

88 points

PAGES 8–9

Survival Work

1) a) S   2) a) 90°
   b) E   b) 180°
   c) NW   c) 270°
   d) W   d) 45°
   e) NE

Math Challenge

1) the church
2) the electricity pylon
3) Flat Rock

PAGES 10–11

Survival Work

1) a) (1, 2)   2) a) White Pool
   b) (3, 3)   b) Lone Tree
   c) 2, 5)   c) Crumbling Cliff

Math Challenge

a) Canal Rocks
b) Wooden Bridge
c) Ling Marsh

PAGES 12–13

Survival Work

The most useful tasks to do within the 4-hour
time limit are building a shelter (150 minutes) and
lighting a fire (45 minutes). These tasks would take
you 195 minutes (3 hours and 15 minutes), leaving
you with 45 minutes to spare.

Math Challenge

1) a) 660 minutes   b) 11 hours
2) hunt for food and light a fire

PAGES 14–15

60 inches = 5 feet		96 inches = 8 feet	
66 inches = 5.5 feet		108 inches = 9 feet	
72 inches = 6 feet		120 inches = 10 feet	
78 inches = 6.5 feet		192 inches = 16 feet	
84 inches = 7 feet		198 inches = 16.5 feet	
90 inches = 7.5 feet		216 inches = 18 feet	

PAGES 16–17

Survival Work

A) 45 inches   C) 65 inches
B) 50 inches   D) 70 inches

Math Challenge

1) a) cylinder
   b) cube
   c) cone
   d) triangular pyramid
   e) triangular prism
   f) sphere
   g) rectangular prism (cuboid)

2) 6 faces, 12 edges (cube)

3) 36 cubic inches

Survival Work

1) 48 ounces
2) More than 1 quart. It is 1.5 quarts.
3) yes
4) 10½ (10.5) quarts

Math Challenge

Fill the 3-quart container and pour the water into the 5-quart container. Fill the 3-quart container again and use it to fill the 5-quart container to the top. You will have 1 quart left in the 3-quart container.

Survival Work

1) leaves	4) 6
2) roots	5) 24
3) 36	6) 6

Math Challenge

168

Survival Work

5 crossings (● = 1 person)

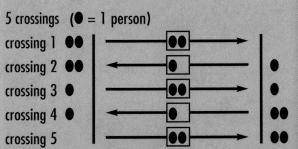

Math Challenge

34 minutes

Survival Work

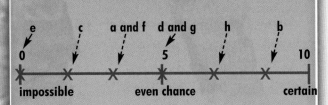

Math Challenge

a) very unlikely, unlikely, likely, or very likely
   (depending on your location)
b) certain
c) very unlikely
d) impossible
e) even chance

Survival Work

1) a) 9 times   b) 6 short blows   c) 3 long blows

2) a) 34 times   15 short blows   19 long blows
   b) 35 times   24 short blows   11 long blows
   c) 24 times   13 short blows   11 long blows

Math Challenge

360 times

GLOSSARY

BOGGY describing wet, spongy, poorly drained ground with marshlike plant life

COMPASS a tool for finding directions, which usually shows eight points using the following abbreviations: N (north), NE (northeast), E (east), SE (southeast), S (south), SW (southwest), W (west), and NW (northwest)

COUNTERCLOCKWISE in the opposite direction from the way a clock's hands turn

EDIBLE safe to eat, not poisonous

FACES the flat surfaces on a solid shape such as a cube or a pyramid

FIRE STARTER a tool that uses a piece of quartz stone, called flint, and a steel rod to create sparks to light a fire

GEOGRAPHIC NORTH the direction of the North Pole, known as "true north"

GRID a network of uniformly spaced horizontal and vertical lines

HYPOTHERMIA a dangerous, and possibly fatal, health condition indicated when a person's body temperature drops far below normal

KINDLING small pieces of wood used to help light a fire

LINE SEGMENT the part of a line on which all points lie between two distinct end points

MAGNETIC NORTH the northerly direction that a compass points to, which is slightly different from geographic north

MORALE the enthusiasm and positive outlook of a group

NAVIGATE find the way, usually by using a map

NORTHERN HEMISPHERE the half of Earth that lies north of the equator. The United States and Canada are both in the Northern Hemisphere.

OUTCROP the part of a usually large rock formation that shows above the surface of the ground

PERIMETER the distance around the edge or boundary of a shape, or a plane figure

PICTOGRAPH a graph or diagram that uses pictures to show information

PRISMS solid figures that have polygon bases of the same size and shape at each end and faces, or sides, that are all parallelograms

PROBABILITY the likelihood or level of possibility that a certain event or outcome will occur

PYLON a tall structure that holds power lines high above the ground

QUICKSAND deep wet sand that, if you step in it, will pull, or suck, you in deeper and deeper until you are buried

RAFTERS the sturdy parallel beams that support a roof

SOUTHERN HEMISPHERE the half of Earth that lies south of the equator. Australia is in the Southern Hemisphere.

SMOKE FLARES canisters that produce a lot of brightly colored smoke and are usually used for signaling

STAGNANT still, not moving or flowing

Measurement Conversions

1 inch = 2.54 centimeters (cm)

1 foot = 0.3048 meter (m)

1 yard = 0.9144 meter (m)

1 mile = 1.609 kilometers (km)

1 ounce = 30 milliliters (ml)

1 quart = 0.95 liter (l)

Fahrenheit (F)° − 32 ÷ 1.8 = Celsius (C)°